NINJA FOODI POSSIBLE PRO COOKER COOKBOOK

21-day Mouthwatering healthy meals for slow cooking, sauteing, searing, baking and more for family-friendly that everyone will love

Nancy C. Bergstrom

Cookbook by Nancy C. Bergstrom

All right reserved. No part of this publication may be reproduced, distributed, or transmitted in any form or by any means, including photocopying, recording, or other electronic or mechanical methods, without the prior written permission of the publisher, except in the case of brief quotations embodied in critical reviews and certain other noncommercial uses permitted by copyright law. Copyright © Nancy C. Bergstrom 2023.

Cookbook by Nancy C. Bergstrom

Cookbook by Nancy C. Bergstrom

TABLE OF CONTENTS

- **INTRODUCTION** 7
- **WHAT IS NINJA FOODI POSSIBLE COOKER** 9
  - Benefits 9
  - Getting Started 10
  - General Safety Instructions 11
  - Cleaning and Maintenance 12
  - Essential tips for using your Ninja Foodi PossibleCooker PRO 12
- **21-DAY MEAL PLAN** 15
- **BREAKFAST** 16
  - PROTEIN CHOCOLATE & PEANUT BUTTER MUFFINS 16
  - BANANA OAT BARS 17
  - BAKED OATS 18
  - CHOCOLATE BAKED OATS 19
  - BANANA BREAD GRANOLA 20
  - TURKISH EGGS 21
  - MUESLI BREAKFAST COOKIES 22
  - CHEDDAR CORN BREAD 24
  - RED VELVET COOKIE 25
  - MILK DINNER ROLLS 27
  - PEAR & CHOCOLATE CRUMBLE 28
- **LUNCH** 30
  - CARROT & CORIANDER SOUP 30
  - STEAK AND ALE PIE 31
  - SAUSAGE AND BEAN HOTPOT 33
  - CREAMY CHICKEN CASSEROLE 34
  - ROOT VEGETABLES WITH BRAISED BEEF IN RED WINE 36
  - SLOW COOKED GAMMON IN CIDER 39
  - VEGETARIAN THREE BEAN CHILI 40
  - BEEF TINGA 41
  - SPICED BRAISED RED CABBAGE WITH APPLE 42
  - BEEF & GUINNESS STEW 43
  - SLOW COOKED LAMB TIKKA MASALA 46
  - SLOW COOKED CHICKEN CORN CHOWDER 48
  - SPICY MEATBALLS WITH GARLIC BROWN RICE NOODLES 50
  - ONION CHUTNEY 51
  - PEA AND MINT SOUP 52
  - ASPARAGUS & PEA RISOTTO 54

SAUSAGE & PEPPER PASTA	55
MINESTRONE SOUP	57

DINNER 59

STEAMED SNOW CRAB LEGS	59
PRO GARLIC CHICKEN	60
MISSISSIPPI POT ROAST	61
POT ROAST	63
SLOW COOKER BEEF HEART STEW	65
LONDON BROIL TACOS	66
SLOW BEEF SHORT RIBS	67
POT ROAST PORK SHOULDER WITH PEPPERS	68
LAMB WITH PUY LENTILS	70
MUSTARD CHICKEN WITH MUSHROOMS AND LEEKS	71
ONE POT CHICKEN & RED RICE PILAF	73
SLOW COOKED VEGGIE CHILLI	76
SLOW COOKED RAGU	77
DATE TAGINE WITH COUSCOUS AND SLOW COOKED SPICED DUCK AND 'QUACKLING'	79
PULLED PORK SLOPPY JOES	81
SLOW COOKED LAMB WITH LAYERED VEGETABLES	82
TOMATO & BASIL LINGUINE	83

DESSERT, SNACKS & APPETIZERS 84

CHOCOLATE SPONGE PUDDING	85
CHEESE & CHIVE SCONES	86
CHOCOLATE ORANGE BROWNIE PIE	87
GREEN TOMATOES CHUTNEY	89
GLUTEN-FREE PAN PIZZA	90
SLOW COOKED MULLED WINE	92
PORTUGUESE PROTEIN RICE PUDDING	93
SPICY CARROT CHUTNEY	94
CHEESECAKE	97

MEASUREMENT CONVERSION 99
BONUS 103
MEAL PLANNER 103

INTRODUCTION

Your Ultimate Guide to Cooking Delicious and Healthy Meals in Half the Time

Are you tired of spending hours in the kitchen cooking? Do you wish there was a way to make delicious and healthy meals without all the hassle? If so, the Ninja Foodi Possible Pro Cooker Cookbook is for you!

This cookbook is packed with over 100 mouth-watering recipes that are all designed to be made in your Ninja Foodi Possible Pro Cooker. From classic comfort foods to healthy and delicious meals, there's something for everyone to enjoy.

But more than just recipes, this cookbook is also a guide to cooking healthy and delicious meals in half the time. With the Ninja Foodi Possible Pro Cooker, you can cook a variety of dishes, from slow-cooked stews to searing and sauteing;" in a fraction of the time it would take on a traditional stovetop or oven.

So what are you waiting for? Grab your apron now and start enjoying delicious and healthy meals in half the time!

Cookbook by Nancy C. Bergstrom

WHAT IS NINJA FOODI POSSIBLE COOKER

The Ninja Foodi PossibleCooker PRO is an 8-in-1 multicooker that can replace 14 kitchen appliances. It is a versatile and powerful appliance that can help you save time and money in the kitchen.

Benefits

Saves Time and Money: The Ninja Foodi PossibleCooker PRO cooks food up to 30% faster than a conventional oven, and it can replace 14 kitchen appliances, so you can save money on counter space and storage.

Versatile: You can cook a wide variety of meals with the Ninja Foodi PossibleCooker PRO, from hearty stews and roasted vegetables to crispy air-fried snacks and decadent desserts.

Easy to Use: The controls are simple and intuitive, and the included recipe guide provides inspiration for delicious meals.

Healthy Cooking: The Ninja Foodi PossibleCooker PRO allows you to cook with less oil and butter, so you can enjoy healthier meals without sacrificing flavor.

Easy to Clean: The nonstick pot and dishwasher-safe parts make cleanup easy.

Getting Started

Unboxing and Setup: Carefully unpack your Ninja Foodi PossibleCooker PRO and remove all packaging materials. Wash the pot, lid, and any other removable parts with warm, soapy water and dry thoroughly before first use.

Choose the Right Function: Decide on the cooking method you want to use. The PossibleCooker PRO offers eight functions: Slow Cook, Sear/Sauté, sous side, Steam, Bake, Roast, Proof, and Keep Warm.

Add Ingredients: Place your ingredients in the pot, ensuring they don't exceed the maximum fill line

Set Cooking Time and Temperature: Select the desired cooking time and temperature using the control panel. Adjust the settings as needed for your chosen recipe.

Start Cooking: Press the Start/Stop button to begin the cooking process. The display will show the remaining cooking time.

Monitor Progress: Keep an eye on your food during cooking to ensure it's cooking evenly and to the desired doneness. if necessary, You may need to adjust the cooking time or temperature.

Flip or Stir (if required): For some cooking methods, such as Sear/Sauté you may need to flip or stir your food midway through cooking to ensure even cooking.

End of Cooking Cycle: When the cooking cycle is complete, the PossibleCooker PRO will beep and switch to the Keep Warm function.

Transfer Food (if necessary): If you're transferring your food to a serving dish, use oven mitts to handle the hot pot and lid.
Enjoy Your Meal: Savor your delicious home-cooked meal!

General Safety Instructions

- Always unplug the PossibleCooker PRO from the power outlet when not in use.
- Never leave the PossibleCooker PRO unattended while it is in operation.
- Do not touch the hot surfaces of the PossibleCooker PRO, including the pot, lid, and handles. However, Use oven mitts when handling hot components.
- Do not place the PossibleCooker PRO on or near a hot stovetop or open flame.
- Do not immerse the PossibleCooker PRO in water or any other liquid.
- Do not use metal utensils in the pot, as they may scratch the nonstick coating. Use wooden or silicone utensils instead.
- Do not fill the pot beyond the maximum fill line.
- Do not overfill the pot, as this could cause spills and splatters.
- Do not place any objects on top of the PossibleCooker PRO while it is in operation.
- Do not use the PossibleCooker PRO for any purpose other than cooking.

Cleaning and Maintenance

- Always allow the PossibleCooker PRO to cool completely before cleaning.
- However, Wash the pot, lid, and other removable parts with warm, soapy water.
- The nonstick pot is dishwasher-safe. However, hand washing is recommended for optimal results and to extend the life of the nonstick coating.
- Do not use abrasive cleaners, scouring pads, or harsh chemicals to clean the PossibleCooker PRO.
- Wipe the exterior of the PossibleCooker PRO with a damp cloth.
- Dry all parts thoroughly before storing the PossibleCooker PRO.

Essential tips for using your Ninja Foodi PossibleCooker PRO

1. Consult the Recipe Guide: Before using the PossibleCooker PRO, always consult the included recipe guide for specific cooking instructions and times. The recipe guide provides detailed instructions for a variety of dishes, from hearty stews and roasted vegetables to crispy air-fried snacks and decadent desserts.

2. Use the Appropriate Function: The PossibleCooker PRO offers eight versatile cooking functions: Slow Cook, Sear/Sauté, Air Fry, Steam, Bake, Roast, Proof, and Keep Warm. Carefully select the appropriate function for the type of dish you are preparing to ensure optimal results.

3. Don't Overcrowd the Pot: When using the Sear/Sauté or Air Fry functions, avoid overcrowding the pot or air fryer basket. Overcrowding can prevent even cooking and lead to less flavorful results.

4. Avoid using too much oil, as this can make the food greasy.

5. Flip or Stir (if required): For some cooking methods, such as Sear/Sauté you may need to flip or stir your food midway through cooking to ensure even cooking. This is especially important for thicker pieces of meat or vegetables.

6. Monitor Progress: Keep an eye on your food during cooking to ensure it's cooking evenly and to the desired doneness. However, You may need to adjust the cooking time or temperature if necessary.

7. Use Oven Mitts: When handling the hot pot or lid, always use oven mitts to protect your hands from burns. The pot and lid can get very hot, especially during cooking.

8. Allow the Pot to Cool: After cooking, allow the pot to cool slightly before washing it with warm, soapy water. The nonstick pot makes cleaning a breeze, but it's important to let it cool first to avoid damaging the coating.

9. Hand Wash for Optimal Results: While the nonstick pot is dishwasher-safe, hand washing is recommended for optimal results and to extend the life of the coating. Hand washing allows you to gently clean the pot without using harsh chemicals or abrasive scrubbing.

10. Store Properly: When not in use, store the PossibleCooker PRO in a clean, dry place. Make sure all parts are completely dry before storing to prevent moisture buildup and potential damage.

21-DAY MEAL PLAN

BREAKFAST

PROTEIN CHOCOLATE & PEANUT BUTTER MUFFINS

PREP TIME:20 MINS.
TOTAL TIME:40 MINS.
SERVES 6 PEOPLE

- 140g fat free Greek yoghurt
- 100g oats
- 1/2 tsp baking powder
- 10g unsweetened cocoa powder
- 50g stevia
- 1 egg
- 6 tsp peanut butter of choice

METHOD

1. Begin by placing the Greek yogurt and oats in the cup of your Ninja Blender and pulsing to combine both ingredients. Rep with the baking powder, cocoa, stevia, and egg.
2. Bake for 15-17 minutes on a prepared baking sheet.
3. Remove the muffins from the pot and set aside to cool before slicing them horizontally across the middle and spreading one teaspoon of peanut butter in the center, then joining the muffins together.

BANANA OAT BARS

PREP TIME:10 MINS.
TOTAL TIME:50 MINS.
SERVES 6 PEOPLE

- 5 ripe bananas
- 360g oats
- 3 tbsp maple syrup
- 1 tsp cinnamon
- A pinch salt

METHOD

1. Blend the bananas and maple syrup in a blender until smooth.
2. In a mixing bowl, combine the banana and maple syrup mixture with the oats, cinnamon, and a sprinkle of salt. Mix thoroughly.
3. Line a baking pot with baking parchment and pour in the mixture, pressing down firmly until compact.
4. Bake for 20 minutes.
5. Allow it to cool for 20 minutes before cutting into bars.

BAKED OATS

PREP TIME: 5 MINS. **TOTAL TIME: 30 MINS.**
SERVES 2 PEOPLE

For the oats
- 100g oats
- 1 banana
- 220ml oat milk
- 30g nut butter
- 30g maple syrup or
- 50g erythritol for sugar free alternative)
- 1 tsp baking powder
- 1/2 tsp salt
- 1 tsp vanilla extract

For the filling
- 120g yoghurt
- 30g protein powder

METHOD
1. Set aside after mixing yogurt and protein powder until creamy.
2. In a blender, combine all of the remaining ingredients until you get a creamy dough.
3. Fill two bowls with 3/4 of the batter.
4. Place your protein topping in the center and cover with the remaining batter.
5. Bake for 20- 25 minutes, then serve this delicious and healthful meal.

CHOCOLATE BAKED OATS

**PREP TIME:10 MINS.   TOTAL TIME:25 MINS.
SERVES 2 PEOPLE**

- 100g oats (1 measuring cup)
- 1 egg
- 250ml almond milk or milk of your choice
- 1 tbsp cacao or cocoa powder
- 1 tbsp maple syrup
- 1 tsp vanilla extract
- 1/2 tsp baking powder
- A handful raspberries
- A handful cacao nibs or chocolate chips
- Flaked almonds to garnish

METHOD

1. In a small deep baking dish, combine the oats, cacao, and baking powder.
2. Whisk in the milk, eggs, vanilla, and honey until smooth.
3. Place the cacao nibs and raspberries over top.
4. Bake the baked oats for 15 minutes at 180° C. Baked oats should be somewhat set with a gooey center. Check the baked oats midway and adjust the settings to your chosen consistency.
5. Allow cooling before removing from the pot using oven gloves, garnishing with flaked almonds, and serving with ice cream or yogurt.

BANANA BREAD GRANOLA

PREP TIME:5 MINS.
TOTAL TIME:25 MINS.
SERVES 4 PEOPLE

- 200g jumbo oats
- 2 bananas
- 60g chopped walnuts
- 3 tbsp maple syrup
- 1 tbsp coconut oil
- 1 tsp cinnamon powder
- 1 tsp vanilla extract
- Pinch of salt

METHOD

1. In a mixing bowl, combine the oats, walnuts, cinnamon, vanilla extract, and a sprinkle of salt.
2. Blend in the banana, maple syrup, and coconut oil until completely smooth.
3. Pour this smooth liquid into the mixing bowl with the dry ingredients and well combine.
4. Line the pot with baking paper and sprinkle the granola mixture on top. Make sure it's tightly packed; this will result in lovely crunchy granola clusters.
5. Bake for about 20 minutes, or until brown. Allow to cool fully before removing from the baking pan.

TURKISH EGGS

**PREP TIME:5 MINS.
TOTAL TIME:15 MINS.
SERVES 2 PEOPLE**

- 4 eggs
- 2 tbsp of cider or white wine vinegar
- 300g yogurt (brought up to room temperature)
- 1 tsp olive oil
- 2 garlic cloves, minced
- 2 tbsp chopped dill(plus some to serve)
- 1 tsp chopped mint
- NADA Salt and pepper to serve
- NADA Toasted bread to serve

For the warm butter
- 30g melted butter
- Pinch chilli flakes
- Pinch cumin
- Pinch paprika

METHOD

1. Turn on the Ninja cooker and choose the slow-cook option on High. Pour 1.5L of water and the vinegar into the pot and set the timer for 10-15 minutes.
2. Break the eggs into ramekins or small dishes to make them simpler to place in the multi cooker later.
3. Lift the cover and make a whirlpool with a spoon, then drop the broken eggs one at a time. Close the cover and boil the eggs for 7-8 minutes, but check the process after 5.
4. While the eggs are cooking, create the sauce by combining the yogurt, olive oil, garlic, dill, mint, and seasoning with salt and pepper in two separate dishes.
5. Then, Season with salt and pepper and keep heating.
6. When the eggs are done, lay them on top of the yogurt sauce and sprinkle with some of the heated butter.
7. Then, garnish with more dill and serve with warm bread.

MUESLI BREAKFAST COOKIES

PREP TIME: 10 MINS.
TOTAL TIME: 40 MINS.
SERVES 9 PEOPLE

- 150g porridge oats
- 150g oat flour
- 4 tbsp maple syrup
- 40g raisins
- 40g dried cranberries
- 30g pumpkin seeds
- 1/2 tsp cinnamon powder
- 1 tsp vanilla extract
- 1 tsp baking powder

- A pinch salt
- For the apple puree
- 3 large cooking apples
- 1 tbsp water

METHOD

1. Begin by peeling and cutting 3 big cooking apples. Remove the core and set it aside. Pour 1 tbsp water in the pot and Allow to slowly cook for about 15 minutes, stirring occasionally. Allow to cool before transferring to purée.
2. Preheat the oven to 160 degrees Celsius.
3. In a mixing dish, combine the oats, oat flour, cinnamon, baking powder, pumpkin seeds, raisins, dried cranberries, and a teaspoon of salt.
4. In a separate dish, combine the maple syrup, apple puree, and vanilla extract.
5. In a mixing bowl, The wet and dry ingredients should be combined. Mix thoroughly. If it's too dry, add a little more apple puree.
6. Line a baking pot with parchment paper.
7. Roll the cookie dough into even-sized balls and put on a baking sheet. You should be able to create 8-10. Flatten into cookie shapes using a spatula.
8. Bake for 12 minutes, or until slightly brown. The cookies will be soft but it will firm up as they cool.
9. Enjoy!

CHEDDAR CORN BREAD

PREP TIME:5 MINS.
TOTAL TIME:30 MINS.
SERVES 8 PEOPLE

- 150g plain flour
- 130g polenta
- 20g granulated sugar
- 2 tsp baking powder
- 2 tsp kosher salt
- 1 medium egg
- 250ml whole milk
- 60ml vegetable oil
- 125g cheddar cheese, grated
- Cooking spray

METHOD

1. Preheat the pot for 5 minutes.
2. Whisk together the flour, polenta, sugar, baking powder, and salt in a medium mixing bowl.
3. To the dry ingredients, mix together the egg, milk, and oil. Stir in the cheese.
4. After 5 minutes, open the cover and spray the pot with cooking spray. Place the baking sheet in the pot.
5. Pour the batter onto a baking sheet.
6. Close the lid. Select BAKE, set the temperature to 180°C, and the timer to 25 minutes. To begin, press the START/STOP button. Bake until the cornbread is golden brown and a wooden toothpick inserted into the center comes out clean.

7. When the cooking is finished, remove the rack containing the pan from the unit and lay it on a cooling rack for 5 minutes before serving. To toast thick slices of cornbread in butter, use the SEAR/SAUTE (MD: HI) option.

RED VELVET COOKIE

PREP TIME:PT-H45M
TOTAL TIME:1H 10 MINS.
SERVES 16 PEOPLE

- 125g butter, softened
- 100g raw cane sugar
- 100g coconut sugar
- 1 large egg
- 1 tsp vanilla extract
- 1-2 tsp high quality gel red food colouring
- 1/2 tsp apple cider vinegar
- 250g gluten-free self-raising flour
- 50g ground almonds
- 2 tbsp unsweetened cocoa or cacao powder
- 1/2 tsp bicarbonate of soda
- Pinch sea salt
- 150g white chocolate chunks/chips

METHOD

1. In a large mixing bowl or stand mixer, cream together the butter and sugars until light and fluffy. Mix in the egg, vanilla, food coloring, and vinegar.
2. In a medium mixing bowl, combine flour, cocoa powder, bicarbonate of soda, and salt. The dry ingredients with the wet ingredients should be mixed until well combined. Set aside 125g of the white chocolate chips for later.
3. Wrap the cookie dough in clingfilm and place it in the freezer for 30 minutes to 1 hour, or until firm.
4. Preheat the oven to 180°C, then oil the pot and put aside.
5. Remove the dough from the freezer and unroll it. Using your fingers, press the dough into an equal layer in the prepared pan.
6. Bake for 22-25 minutes, or until set. On the surface, There should be a few cracks.
7. Remove from the heat and let aside for 5 to 10 minutes before gently pressing the remaining chocolate pieces into the surface of the cookie. Serve warm with ice cream if preferred.

Notes:

1. If white chocolate is too sweet for you, use milk or dark chocolate chips.
2. The cookies may be kept in an airtight container at room temperature for up to a week or in the freezer for up to 6 weeks. If frozen, Thaw in the refrigerator overnight.

Cookbook by Nancy C. Bergstrom

MILK DINNER ROLLS

PREP TIME:1H 20 MINS. TOTAL TIME:1H 40 MINS. SERVES. 8 PEOPLE

- 350-400ml whole milk
- 100g butter, plus extra for greasing
- 700g strong white flour, plus extra for kneading
- 10g easy blend yeast
- 1 tsp salt
- 1 tsp sugar
- 1 small egg, beaten with 1 tablespoon water

METHOD
1. Pour milk into the pan. Heat until tepid. Clean and butter the pan.
2. In a large mixing bowl, combine the flour, yeast, salt, sugar, and butter. After then, Rub the butter into the flour with your fingers. Gradually mix in the milk until the mixture comes together.
3. Then, Turn the dough out onto a floured board and knead until smooth and elastic. Divide into 12 balls and put in a circle in the pan. Cover the pan with a cover and set aside in a warm place to rise until doubled in size. (About 1-2 hours).
4. Preheat the oven to 220°C.

- Brush the egg mixture on the rolls. After then, Bake for 20-25 minutes, or until golden brown. Remove from the pan and cool gently on a wire rack. Then break apart and serve.

PEAR & CHOCOLATE CRUMBLE

PREP TIME:15 MINS.
TOTAL TIME:55 MINS.
SERVES 6 PEOPLE

- 700g pears
- 2 tbsp maple syrup
- 2 tbsp water
- 1/2 tsp ground cinnamon
- 1/2 tsp ground ginger
- 1/2 tsp vanilla extract
- 1/2 juice of lemon

For the crumble
- 175g gluten free oats
- 60g vegan butter, room temp
- 45ml maple syrup
- 1 tsp vanilla extract
- 20g cacao powder
- 30g ground almonds
- 20g dark chocolate chips

METHOD

1. Firstly, Peel and core the pears, then cut them into quarter slices.
2. Pour in the diced pears, maple syrup, water, cinnamon, ginger, vanilla, and lemon.
3. Then, Cover and cook for 15 minutes, stirring occasionally.
4. To prepare the crumble, combine all of the ingredients, except the vegan butter, in a mixing bowl.
5. Rub the vegan butter into the crumble mixture with your hands until it is equally combined.
6. Pour the cooked pears into the pot.
7. Crumble mixture on top
8. Bake for 25 minutes.
9. Serve with dairy-free yogurt or ice cream.

LUNCH

CARROT & CORIANDER SOUP

PREP TIME:15 MINS. COOK TIME:25 MINS.
SERVES 6 PEOPLE

- 2 tbsp olive oil
- 1 large onion, finely sliced
- 15g bunch fresh coriander, chopped, divided
- 2 tsp ground coriander
- 1 tsp ground cumin
- 1 garlic clove, peeled and crushed
- 250g potato, peeled and diced
- 750g carrots, sliced
- 1.4L vegetable stock
- Salt and freshly ground black pepper, as desired
- 6 tbsp crème fraîche

METHOD
1. Remove the pot's cover. Set the dial to SEAR/SAUTÉ, the temperature to HI, then hit START/STOP to begin preheating. Allow the unit to preheat for 5 minutes.
2. Add the oil and onion to the the pan. Covered, cook, for 5 minutes, stirring periodically.

3. Take off the lid. Add half of the fresh coriander and the other ingredients, except the crème fraiche, to the the pan. Stir to mix, then cover with the lid. Cook for 10-15 minutes, or until the carrots and potatoes are soft.
4. When the soup has finished simmering, remove the cover and set it aside to cool somewhat. Transfer the cooled soup to a blender and puree until smooth. Return the puréed soup to the pot to reheat.
5. Stir in the remaining coriander, saving a few leaves for garnishes. Serve in soup bowls topped with crème fraîche and coriander.

STEAK AND ALE PIE

PREP TIME:15 MINS.
COOK TIME:3H 30 MINS
SERVES 6 PEOPLE

- 2 tbsp olive oil
- 800g stewing or braising steak,
- cut into 4cm cubes
- 35g plain flour
- Salt, as desired
- Ground black pepper, as desired
- 2 medium white onions, peeled, finely diced

- 2 carrots, peeled, sliced
- 200g chestnut mushrooms, cleaned, halved
- 2 celery sticks, sliced
- 1 garlic clove, peeled, crushed
- 1 tbsp tomato purée
- 1 tbsp Worcestershire sauce
- 1 tsp English mustard
- 500ml brown ale
- 2 tsp dried mixed herbs
- 2 bay leaves
- 350g puff pastry
- 1 large egg
- 1 tbsp milk

METHOD

1. Remove the pot's cover. Set the dial to SEAR/SAUTÉ, the temperature to HI, then hit START/STOP to begin preheating. Allow the unit to preheat for 5 minutes.
2. Toss the steak with flour, salt, and pepper in a large mixing bowl. Shake any excess flour off the steak and set aside. In the pot, combine the oil and the steak. Cook, uncovered, for 10 minutes, stirring periodically. When the steak has browned, remove it with a slotted spoon and put it aside.
3. In the pot, combine all the ingredients except the puff pastry, egg, and milk. Add the steak and any juices. Stir to mix, then cover with the lid.
4. Set the dial to SLOW COOK, the temperature to HI, the time to 3 hours, and the START/STOP button to begin cooking.
5. When the filling is done, stir it to make sure it isn't sticking to the bottom of the pot, then remove the bay leaves and set aside to cool somewhat. Meanwhile, preheat the oven to 220°C.

6. Roll out puff pastry to suit the size of the pot, then cut to fit. Place the puff pastry on top of the steak and ale filling. Crimp the crust along the pot's sides. Cut four slits in the top of the crust with a knife.
7. In a small bowl, the egg and milk should be combined. Brush the egg mixture over the top of the crust. Place the whole pot (without the cover) in the oven for 30 minutes, or until the crust is golden brown.
8. When the pie is done cooking, serve it immediately.

SAUSAGE AND BEAN HOTPOT

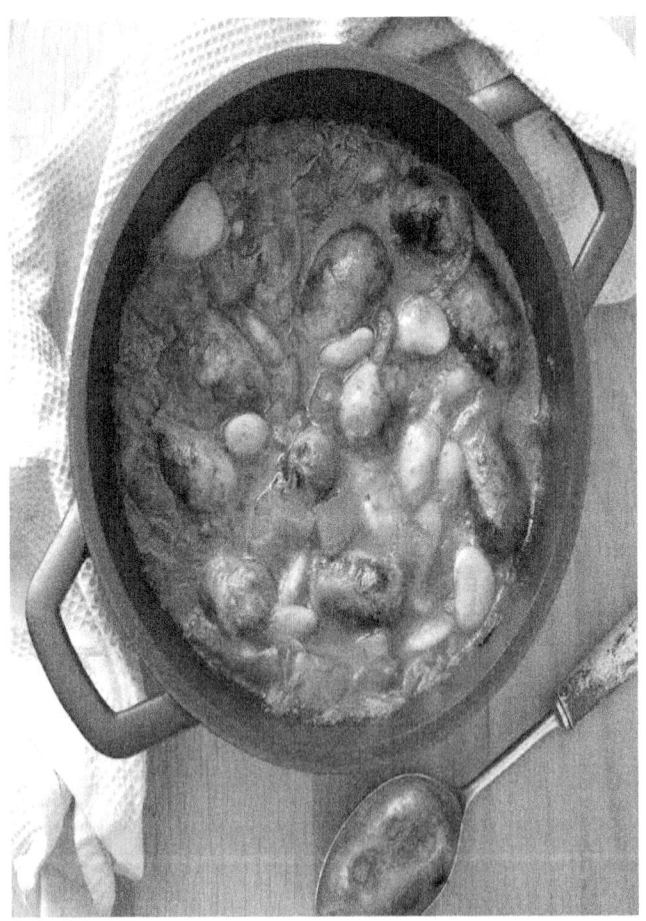

**PREP TIME:15 MINS.
COOK TIME:3 HOURS
SERVES 8 PEOPLE**

- 130g lardon cubes
- 800g pork sausages
- 2 red onions, peeled and diced
- 2 celery sticks, sliced
- 2 garlic cloves, peeled and crushed
- 2 tbsp sundried tomato purée
- 1 x 400g can chopped tomatoes
- 1 x 400g can butter beans,
- drained and rinsed

- 200ml red wine
- 1 tbsp sweet paprika
- 1 tsp dried oregano
- 2 tbsp fresh flat leaf parsley, chopped
- 2 bay leaves
- Salt, as desired
- Ground black pepper, as desired

METHOD
1. Add all of the ingredients to the pot. Stir to mix, then cover with the lid.
2. Set the dial to BRAISE, the temperature to HI, the time to 3 hours, and the START/STOP button to begin cooking.
3. Remove the cover after the cooking is finished. Remove the bay leaf and mix in the remaining ingredients. Serve immediately.

CREAMY CHICKEN CASSEROLE

**PREP TIME:15 MINS.
COOK TIME:2 HOURS
SERVES 5 PEOPLE**

- 8 x 150g bone in, skin-on chicken thighs
- Salt, as desired
- Ground black pepper, as desired
- 130g smoked pancetta cubes
- 150g shallots, peeled and cut in half if large

- 125g chestnut mushrooms, cleaned, halved
- 2 garlic cloves, peeled, crushed
- 200ml white wine
- 200ml chicken stock
- 1 tsp dried tarragon
- 2 tsp corn flour
- 1-2 tbsp cold water
- 3-4 tbsp crème fraîche
- 2 tbsp fresh flat leaf parsley, chopped

METHOD

- Set the dial to SEAR/SAUTÉ, the temperature to HI, then hit START/STOP to begin preheating. Allow the unit to preheat for 5 minutes.
- Season the chicken on both sides with salt and pepper while the unit is heating.
- When the pancetta and shallots are ready, add them to the the pot. Cook, uncovered, for 5 minutes, or until browned, stirring occasionally.
- After 5 minutes, remove the pancetta and shallots using a slotted spoon and leave aside.
- Place the chicken in the the pot, skin side down, and cook for 10 minutes, or until brown on both sides. Add mushrooms, garlic, wine, stock, tarragon, salt & pepper, pancetta, and shallots to the the pot. Stir everything together. Stir to mix, then cover with the lid.
- To begin cooking, set the dial to BRAISE, the temperature to HI, the timer to 1 hour 45 minutes, and the START/STOP button.
- In a small mixing bowl, combine corn flour and water. Remove the cover after 15 minutes and stir the corn flour mixture into the dish to thicken.

- When the chicken is done cooking, remove the cover and set it aside for 5 minutes to cool. Stir in the crème fraîche and parsley. Serve hot.

ROOT VEGETABLES WITH BRAISED BEEF IN RED WINE

**PREP TIME:15 MINS.
COOK TIME:3H 30 MINS
SERVES 6 PEOPLE**

- 2 tbsp olive oil, divided
- 4 x 200g braising steaks
- 30g plain flour
- Salt, as desired
- Ground black pepper, as desired
- 2 medium white onions, finely sliced
- 2 celery sticks, 1cm slices
- 200g Chantenay carrots, cut in half if large
- 250g sweet potato, peeled and diced into 4cm chunks
- 300g parsnips peeled and diced into 4cm chunks
- 1 garlic clove, peeled, crushed

- 1 tbsp tomato purée
- 1 tsp English mustard
- 250ml beef stock
- 250ml red wine
- 2 tsp dried thyme
- 1 bay leaf

METHOD

1. Season the beef on both sides with salt and pepper, then coat with flour.
2. Remove the pot's cover. Set the dial to SEAR/SAUTÉ, the temperature to HI, then hit START/STOP to begin preheating. Allow the unit to preheat for 5 minutes.
3. Add 1 tablespoon oil and the steaks to the pot. Cook, uncovered, for 10 minutes, or until browned on both sides.
4. Add the remaining 1 tablespoon of oil and all of the additional ingredients to the the pot. Season with salt and pepper to taste. Stir to mix, then cover with the lid.
5. Set the dial to BRAISE, the temperature to HI, the time to 3 hours, and the START/STOP button to begin cooking.
6. When the cooking is finished, gently remove the cover, remove the bay leaf, and set the dish aside to cool for 5 minutes before serving.

SLOW COOKED GAMMON IN CIDER

PREP TIME: 10 MINS.
TOTAL TIME: 6H 10 MINS
SERVES 6 PEOPLE

- 1.4kg unsmoked gammon joint
- 1 onion, peeled, quartered
- 1 carrot, peeled, thickly sliced
- 1 stick celery, halved
- 1 tsp black peppercorns
- 2 bay leaves
- 300ml dry cider

For the glaze

- 2 tbsp wholegrain mustard
- 1 tbsp maple syrup

METHOD

1. Remove the pot's cover. Arrange the veggies, peppercorns, and bay leaves around the gammon in the pot. Pour in the cider and cover with the lid.
2. Set the dial to SLOW COOK, the temperature to LO, the time to 6 hours, and the START/STOP button to begin cooking.
3. Meanwhile, combine the mustard and maple syrup in a small bowl. Set aside for later
4. Allow to gently cool before removing the gammon and discarding the veggies and liquid. Remove the pot
5. Preheat the oven to 200°C.
6. Score the gammon after removing the skin. Brush the gammon with the mustard mixture all over. Replace in the pot. Bake for 20-30 minutes or until golden brown and glazed. Serve hot or cold.

VEGETARIAN THREE BEAN CHILI

PREP TIME:15 MINS
COOK TIME:6 HOURS
SERVES 12 PEOPLE

- 1 onion, peeled, diced
- 2 carrots, peeled, chopped
- 3 celery stalks, chopped
- 3 cloves garlic, peeled, chopped
- 1 x 400g can chickpeas, drained and rinsed
- 1 x 400g can black beans, drained and rinsed
- 1 x 400g can kidney beans, drained and rinsed
- 1 x 25g packet taco seasoning
- 2 tbsp adobo chili paste
- 800g tomato puree
- 2 x 400g cans chopped tomatoes
- 1L water
- Sea salt, as desired
- Ground black pepper, as desired

TOPPINGS (optional)
- Sour cream
- Grated Cheddar cheese
- Fresh chopped coriander

METHOD

1. Put everything in the pot. Stir to combine, then cover with the lid.
2. SLOW COOK, HI, 6 hours, and START/STOP to begin cooking.
3. When the cooking is finished, remove the cover and stir to mix the ingredients. Serve chili immediately with chosen toppings.

BEEF TINGA

PREP TIME:15 MINS.
COOK TIME:8 HOURS.
SERVES 8 PEOPLE

- 1.3kg silverside
- 2 tsp ground cumin
- 1 tsp ground cinnamon
- 2 medium onions, peeled, sliced
- 2 garlic cloves, peeled, crushed
- 2 x 400g cans chopped tomatoes
- 4 tbsp chipotle chilli sauce
- 2 bay leaves
- Salt, as desired
- Ground black pepper, as desired
- Wraps, to serve
- Salsa, to serve

METHOD
1. Season beef with cumin, and cinnamon, and season to taste.
2. Add onions, garlic, diced tomatoes, chipotle chili sauce, bay leaves, and season to taste. Spoon sauce over beef to completely coat it. Cover with the lid.
3. Set the dial to SLOW COOK, the temperature to LO, the timer to 8 hours, and the START/STOP button to begin cooking.
4. Check the beef at the end of cooking to determine whether it's soft enough to shred; if not, flip the beef over and continue cooking for another hour.
5. When the beef is done, remove the bay leaves and place them on a board. Shred with two forks. Return the beef to the sauce and serve hot with wraps and salsa.

SPICED BRAISED RED CABBAGE WITH APPLE

**PREP TIME:20 MINS.
COOK TIME:1H 30 MINS.
SERVES 6 PEOPLE**

- 1 shallot, peeled, finely diced
- 900g red cabbage,
- shredded with core removed
- Zest and juice of 1 orange
- 1 cinnamon stick
- 200ml water
- 3 tbsp red wine vinegar
- 1 tbsp granulated sugar
- 2 star anise
- 2 bay leaves

- Salt, as desired
- Ground black pepper, as desired

METHOD
1. Heat Ninja Foodi on medium-high. Bring all of the ingredients to a boil and mix to combine. Reduce heat to low, cover with a lid, and cook for 1 hour 30 minutes, or until softened, stirring periodically.
2. When done, serve as an accompaniment to turkey.

BEEF & GUINNESS STEW

PREP TIME:20 MINS.
TOTAL TIME:2H 50 MINS
SERVES 6 PEOPLE

For the beef stew
- 2 tbsp olive oil
- 1kg braising beef, cut into 2.5cm cubes
- 2 medium onions, each cut into 8 wedges
- 2 carrots, peeled, cut into 2.5cm pieces
- 1 leek, cut into 2.5cm pieces
- 200g chestnut mushrooms, halved or quartered
- 4 garlic cloves, finely chopped

- 6 sprigs of fresh thyme
- 2 tbsp tomato puree
- 3 tbsp plain flour, seasoned
- 440ml Guinness
- 750ml beef stock
- Salt
- Ground black pepper

For the dumplings
- 150g self-raising flour
- 75g suet, vegetarian or beef
- 2 tbsp fresh chopped parsley
- 2 tbsp horseradish sauce, or 2 tsp fresh grated horseradish

METHOD
1. Preheat the oven to 180°C.
2. Place the Ninja Possible Pot on a medium heat setting and let the oil warm for around 1 minute.
3. Cook the beef in batches until browned, approximately 6 minutes. Place each batch on a plate and put aside.
4. Sauté the onions, carrots, mushrooms, and leeks in the pot for approximately 10 minutes, or until softened. Cook for 5 minutes more after adding the garlic and thyme.
5. Return the beef to the pot with the veggies. Season with salt and pepper to taste. Stir in the flour until well combined. Cook for another 8 minutes.
6. Bring the Guinness and stock to a simmer in the pot. Cook for 2 hours when it has started to simmer.
7. Prepare the dumplings while the stew cooks. Combine the dumpling ingredients in a large mixing bowl. Add cold water a tablespoon at a time to the ingredients until a thick dough forms. Refrigerate the dough in 8 balls until required.

8. After 1 hour and 45 minutes, take the stew from the pot and examine the beef for tenderness. You want it to be fork tender. Continue cooking if the beef is not tender, and check after 2 hours.
9. When the beef is soft, place the dumplings on top of the stew. Bake for 20 minutes, then serve the stew with buttery potatoes and greens.

SLOW COOKED LENTIL RAGU

PREP TIME: 10 MINS.   TOTAL TIME: 4H 10 MINS.

SERVES 4 PEOPLE

- 1 tbsp garlic infused olive oil
- 1 stalk celery
- 1 large carrot, peeled
- 2 tbsp chopped fresh chives (or 1 onion)
- 1 tin green lentils, rinsed and drained
- 1 tin chopped tomatoes
- 1 vegetable stock pot
- 1 tsp paprika
- 1 tsp mixed herbs
- 120ml red wine
- Salt & pepper
- 300g gluten free tagliatelle
- Fresh basil (optional to garnish)

- Parmesan (optional to garnish)

METHOD

1. Select the sear/sauté option on medium heat, then add the oil.
2. Finely slice the celery and carrot and add them to the foodi along with the chives (or onion).
3. Saute for 5 minutes
4. Stir in the lentils, tomatoes, stock pot, paprika, herbs, and wine.
5. Select the slow cooker option on high, and set the timer for 4 hours.
6. Once cooked, Open and season with salt and pepper to suit.
7. Cook the tagliatelle according to package directions.
8. Combine the cooked tagliatelle with the ragu.
9. Serve with fresh basil and parmesan (if using).

SLOW COOKED LAMB TIKKA MASALA

PREP TIME:10 MINS.
TOTAL TIME:3H 30 MINS.
SERVES 2 PEOPLE

- 350g diced lamb
- 4 tbsp full fat Greek yoghurt
- 1 brown onion, finely diced
- 1 red chilli, sliced
- 400g tin chopped tomatoes
- 400g tin coconut milk

- 1 tsp chilli flakes
- 2 tbsp garam masala
- 1/2 tsp ground coriander
- 2 tsp ground cumin
- 2 tsp garlic puree
- 1 tsp ground ginger
- 1 tsp salt
- 2 tbsp olive oil
- For garnishing chopped fresh coriander
- To serve rice or naan bread

METHOD

1. Add 1x Tbsp Garam Masala, 1 Tsp Ground Cumin, 12 Tsp Ground Coriander, and salt to a mixing basin, followed by the Greek Yoghurt, and then blend the ingredients.
2. Mix in the lamb pieces well. Allow this to marinade for at least 1 hour, and preferably longer. Making this ahead of time helps improve the flavors.
3. To begin making your curry sauce, utilize the SAUTE function (high heat setting). Warm the olive oil and sauté the onions until softened/slightly browned.
4. Continue to sauté for another 2 minutes after adding the sliced red chili and chili flakes.
5. Heat for 1 minute after adding the Garlic Puree and Ground Ginger.
6. Then add the diced tomatoes and coconut milk and bring to a boil.
7. Once cooking, add the lamb and yogurt marinade and mix thoroughly.
8. Close the cover and set the Slow Cooking setting to High for 3 hours.
9. Allow your curry to slowly simmer for this amount of time, stirring periodically.

10. After this time, your curry sauce should be thick and a deep orange color.
11. It should be Serve with your curry garnished with coriander and your choice of side, such as rice or naan bread.

SLOW COOKED CHICKEN CORN CHOWDER

PREP TIME:15 MINS.   TOTAL TIME:3H 15 MINS.
SERVES 6 PEOPLE

- 4-5 medium potatoes
- 300g chicken breast
- 2L vegetable stock
- 300g corn kernels
- 2 carrots (diced)
- 1 small onion
- 2 tbsp cooking oil
- 3 tbsp flour
- 1/2 cup single cream
- 100g bacon rashes
- 1 clove garlic
- 1 tbsp pepper

For the garnish
- Handful chives
- Fried bacon
- Cheese of your choice (optional)

METHOD

1. Select the sear/sauté option on your Ninja Foodi, add the bacon, and fry until crispy - generally approximately 5 minutes. Once the bacon is crispy, remove it.
2. Sauté the chopped onion, garlic, and 2 tbsp olive oil for 2-3 minutes, or until golden brown but not burnt. Mix with 2 tbsp of flour.
3. Add all of the veggies to the cooking pot, along with the stock, salt, pepper, and chicken.
4. Set the timer for 3 hours on the Slow Cook mode, high heat.
5. When the timer goes off, add 1/2 cup of single cream and mix thoroughly until combined.
6. Use a potato masher to break down the potatoes and the chicken (the chicken should now come apart easily). Optionally, take 1 cup of the soup, let it cool, and add to a blender. Blend until smooth, then combine with the soup to thicken.
7. Serve with the fried bacon, fresh herbs, chives, and cheese, if desired.

SPICY MEATBALLS WITH GARLIC BROWN RICE NOODLES

PREP TIME:10 MINS.
TOTAL TIME:3H 30 MINS
SERVES 4 PEOPLE

For the meatballs
- 500g pork or beef mince meat
- Salt and pepper
- 2 tbsp sesame oil
- 1 tsp chopped ginger
- 1/2 cup breadcrumbs
- 1 egg
- 1 tbsp minced garlic

For the chilli sauce
- 1/3 cup brown sugar
- 1/3 cup apple cider vinegar or white vinegar or rice vinegar
- 1 1/2 cup water
- 1 tsp chili flakes
- 1 tbsp minced garlic
- 1 tbsp soy sauce
- 1 tsp salt
- 2 dried chillies (optional)
- Extras
- Baby bokchoi
- Brown rice noodles, cooked
- Sesame seeds
- Fresh coriander

- 1 tbsp cornflour
- 3 tbsp all purpose flour

METHOD

1. In a large mixing bowl, combine all of the meatball ingredients until well combined.
2. Then, form into balls using a small ice cream scoop.
3. Roll each ball in all-purpose flour.
4. Set your Ninja to sear, add 1 tablespoon of oil, and cook the meatballs for a minute or two.
5. Mix in all of the sauce ingredients until completely mixed.
6. Change the setting to the slow cook option. Select medium heat and 3 hours. Close the lid and let it cook.
7. When it's finished, combine cornflour with 2-3 tbsp water and add it to the meatballs. The sauce will thicken.
8. Serve with cooked noodles and your favorite veggies or seeds. Garnish with fresh coriander

ONION CHUTNEY

PREP TIME:20 MINS.
TOTAL TIME:4H 25 MINS.
SERVES 20 PEOPLE

- 1kg onions, peeled, quartered and sliced into 1mm slices
- 2 tbsp oil
- 150ml marsala wine
- 70ml balsamic vinegar

- 100g raisins
- 2 tbsp brown sugar
- ½ tsp chilli flakes
- ½ tsp salt
- ½ tsp pepper

METHOD

1. Set the SEAR/SAUTÉ to HIGH. To begin, press the START/STOP button. Allow 5 minutes for the oven to preheat.
2. Sauté onions in oil for 5 minutes. Then add marsala wine and cook for another 10 minutes.
3. Stir in the rest of the ingredients.
4. Set SLOW COOK to HIGH. Set the timer to 4 hours. To begin, press the START/STOP button.
5. When cooking is finished, take the pot from the unit and set it aside to cool. Pour chutney into jars. After then, Refrigerate for up to a week or freeze for up to a year.

PEA AND MINT SOUP

PREP TIME:20 MINS.
COOK TIME:30 MINS
SERVES 8 PEOPLE

- 2 tbsp oil
- 1 bunch of spring onions, sliced
- 1 potato, peeled and cubed
- 2 garlic cloves, crushed

- 1.5L hot vegetable stock
- 750g frozen peas, thawed
- 50g fresh pea shoots, save some for serving
- 10g fresh mint leaves freshly ground black pepper and
- Salt as desired
- Crème fraîche or natural yogurt to garnish

METHOD

1. Add oil to pot. On medium heat preheat oil for a few minutes before adding onion. Select BRAISE Cook with the lid on for a few minutes to soften before adding potato and garlic. Cook with the lid on for 2 minutes more.
2. Add the hot stock and thawed peas. Bring to a boil and then simmer. Once simmering, add the mint leaves, pea shoots and seasoning. Cook for 5-10 minutes.
3. Allow the soup to cool slightly before pureeing it with a food processor or blender until smooth.
4. Pour the soup back into the pot. Bring the soup back to a slow simmer, turn off the heat.
5. Serve in bowls with a teaspoon of crème fraîche or yogurt and garnish with pea shoots.

ASPARAGUS & PEA RISOTTO

PREP TIME:10 MINS
COOK TIME:40 MINS
SERVES 4 PEOPLE

- 1 tbsp olive oil
- 40g butter, divided
- 1 onion, peeled, finely diced
- 200g asparagus stalks, trimmed, cut into 2cm lengths
- 300g arborio or Carnaroli risotto rice
- 200ml dry white wine
- 900ml hot vegetable stock
- 200g frozen peas, thawed
- 60g finely grated Parmesan or vegetarian equivalent, plus extra for serving
- Salt, as desired
- Ground black pepper, as desired

METHOD

1. Preheat for 2 minutes.
2. Add oil and 20g butter. Once the butter is melted, add the onion and asparagus. Select BRAISE and Cook for 5 minutes, stirring regularly until the onion and asparagus soften.

3. Add the rice and stir to combine, cooking for 2 minutes. Add the wine and bring the mixture to a simmer, stirring regularly, for 2 to 3 minutes, or until almost all of the wine has evaporated off.
4. Gradually add stock to the pan one ladle full at a time. After, Mix stock into rice until absorbed, then add more. Continue this process for about 25 mins, until most of the stock has been absorbed and the rice is cooked but still slightly al dente.
5. Add the peas, remaining butter, Parmesan, salt, and pepper, and gently mix to combine.
6. When cooking is complete, serve risotto immediately with extra Parmesan as desired.

SAUSAGE & PEPPER PASTA

PREP TIME:15 MINS.
TOTAL TIME:1H 5 MINS
SERVES 6 PEOPLE

- 1 tbsp olive oil
- 10 pork sausages
- 1 onion, sliced
- 1 red pepper, deseeded and sliced
- 1 green pepper, deseeded and sliced
- 1 garlic clove, sliced
- 1 tsp fennel seeds
- ½ tsp hot-smoked paprika
- Pinch dried chilli flakes
- freshly ground black pepper and salt

- 1 can (400g) chopped tomatoes
- 1 tbsp tomato purée
- 1 tsp dried herbs
- 600ml chicken stock
- 200g dried penne pasta
- 2 tbsp crème fraîche or natural yogurt
- 2 tbsp grated Parmesan, plus extra;
  To serve 10 torn fresh basil leaves

METHOD

1. Select sear/saute to Heat the oil in the pot for 1-2 minutes then add sausages and brown them on all sides. This may take a few minutes.
2. Remove sausages from the pot and reserve. Add the onions and peppers, select BRAISE, and cook with lid on for 5 minutes until soft.
3. Meanwhile, slice the sausages on the slant into 3 and add back to the pot with garlic, fennel, smoked paprika, and chili flakes. Then Cook, with the lid off for 2 minutes.
4. Add tomatoes, tomato purée, dried herbs, and stock. Replace the lid and bring the pot contents to a boil before simmering for 10 minutes.
5. Stir in the dry pasta, bring to a boil, then cover and cook on a LO simmer for 10-12 minutes, stirring occasionally. When the pasta is nearly done, add the crème fraîche, Parmesan, and basil leaves, if desired.

MINESTRONE SOUP

PREP TIME:20 MINS.
TOTAL TIME:2 HOURS
SERVES 8 PEOPLE

- 2 tbsp olive oil
- 1 large onion, diced
- 2 carrots, diced
- 1 large leek, chopped
- 2 sticks celery, diced
- 2 garlic cloves, crushed
- 2 courgettes, chopped
- 5 dark cabbage leaves, shredded
- 2 cans (400g each) cannellini or borlotti beans, drained
- 2 cans (400g each) chopped tomatoes
- 1 1/2L vegetable stock
- 1 tsp salt
- 1/2 tsp ground black pepper
- 130g dried pasta,
- shape of choice fresh basil leaves, roughly chopped
- Grated Parmesan or vegetarian equivalent, to serve, optional

METHOD

1. Pour olive oil into the Ninja Possible Pot. Allow to preheat for 1 minute.

2. Sauté the onion, carrots, leek, and celery in the pot for 10 minutes on a LO, or until the veggies are softened. Cook for 5 minutes more after adding the garlic and courgette.
3. Stir in the beans, diced tomatoes, and cabbage, as well as the stock, salt, and pepper. Select BRAISE Bring the soup to a simmer and cook for another 40 minutes.
4. Add the pasta to the soup, along with half of the basil, and cook for 12-15 minutes, or until the pasta is tender.
5. Serve immediately in bowls, topped with the remaining basil and, if preferred sprinkle with Parmesan.

DINNER

STEAMED SNOW CRAB LEGS

yield: 2
prep time: 5 MINUTES
cook time: 13 MINUTES
INGREDIENTS
- 1 ½ lb pre cooked frozen snow crab legs
- 2 lemons
- 3 tablespoon old bay seasoning
- (or to your liking)
- 2 cups water
- Melted butter for dipping (optional)

INSTRUCTIONS
1. Insert a steamer rack (or any other rack that will fit) into the pot. Fill the pot with water.
2. Put the snow crab legs in the pot. Season the legs well with old bay seasoning. Add half of the lemon. Close the lid.
3. Set your steamer to 13 minutes. Squeeze extra lemon juice on top after the dish is done. Serve with melted butter.

PRO GARLIC CHICKEN

yield: 6 prep time: 10 MINUTES cook time: 2 HOURS

INGREDIENTS
- 1 whole chicken, cut in to parts
- 1 onion, quartered
- 6 garlic cloves, roughly chopped
- 1 tablespoon salt
- 1 tablespoon black pepper
- 1 tablespoon smoked paprika
- 1 tablespoon garlic powder
- 1 tablespoon onion powder
- couple springs of fresh rosemary
- 1 teaspoon cumin
- 1 teaspoon chicken bullion
- 1 tablespoon olive oil

INSTRUCTIONS
1. Sear the oil in the Possible cooker. Sear the chicken pieces on each side until browned. Add the onion and garlic.
2. Close the lid after adding all of the spices. Cook for 40 minutes, stirring periodically, on SAUTE.
3. Cook for another hour after pressing Braise.

NOTES:
- ☐ For a set-and-forget dish, saute the chicken for 5 minutes (for color) before slow cooking on HIGH for 2-3 hours.
- ☐ To prevent the chicken breast from drying out, remove it from the saucepan after the searing step in the original recipe. Wrap in foil and set aside once the cooking is finished.
- ☐ Add BBQ sauce for a great BBQ chicken taste.
- ☐ There is no need to add any water or broth to the recipes since the chicken will provide adequate juice when cooking.

MISSISSIPPI POT ROAST

yield: 5   prep time: 5 MINUTES   cook time: 4 HOURS

INGREDIENTS
- 3 lb beef chuck roast
- ½ onion chopped
- 3 cloves garlic chopped
- 8 pepperoncini
- ½ cup pepperoncini juice
- 1 packet Au Jus powdered mix
- 1 packet Ranch seasoning mix
- 4 tablespoon unsalted butter (half a stick)

INSTRUCTIONS
1. Add all of the ingredients to your Possible cooker.
2. Close the lid and press the Slow Cooker button. Set the time and temperature to 4 hours on HIGH and 8 hours on LOW.
3. Watch for steam when you open the lid. With two forks, shred the meat.
4. Serve with white rice, mashed potatoes, or noodles.

NOTES FOR LEFTOVERS:
- Cover the Ninja Foodi Possible cooker pot with the lid (the same size lid as your other pots will work). Refrigerate for up to three days. Reheat in the same pot using the SAUTE button.

POT ROAST

yield: 5. prep time: 10 MINS cook time: 4 HOURS

INGREDIENTS
- 1 ½ lb chuck roast
- 1 onion, chopped
- 3 celery ribs, chopped
- 2 cups baby carrots
- 1 lb baby potatoes
- 2 tablespoon Worcestershire sauce
- 2 cups beef broth
- 3 sprigs fresh thyme
- 1 tablespoon olive oil
- 1 tablespoon black pepper
- 1 teaspoon salt

- 1 tablespoon garlic powder

INSTRUCTIONS

1. Using the SEAR function, heat the oil in the possible cooker. Season the meat with salt, pepper, and garlic powder and set it in the hot oil. On each side it should be cook for 3 minutes.
2. Add the onions, carrots, celery, and potatoes. Add the broth and Worcestershire sauce. Thyme is optional.
3. Close the cover and cook for 4 hours on HIGH or 8 hours on LOW.

NOTES:

- To keep leftover pot roast, let it cool to room temperature before transferring to an airtight container and refrigerating for up to 3-4 days.
- To reheat, put the appropriate quantity in a microwave-safe dish and microwave until warmed through, or cook it on the stove over medium heat, stirring periodically, until hot. If the dish seems dry, add a splash of broth or water while warming.

SLOW COOKER BEEF HEART STEW

yield: 4 prep time: 7 MINS
cook time: 5 HOURS

INGREDIENTS
- 1 lb beef heart
- ⅓ chopped onion
- ½ cup water or broth
- 1 teaspoon salt
- 4 cloves garlic

INSTRUCTIONS
1. Wash the beef heart in cool water. Remove any extra fat from the heart and cut it into 1 inch chunks. Place in a slow cooker.
2. Finely chop the onion and garlic and add to the cooker. If used, add some water or broth. Season with salt.
3. Set the slow cooker on high for roughly 4-5 hours or low for 8-9 hours.
4. When finished, stir in the cilantro.

LONDON BROIL TACOS

yield: 6 prep time: 5 MINS cook time: 8 HOURS

INGREDIENTS
- 3 lb london broil steak
- 2 tablespoon adobo sauce
- 3 garlic cloves, minced
- 2 teaspoons salt
- 2 teaspoons ground cumin
- 1 teaspoon oregano
- 1 teaspoon ground black pepper
- 2 tablespoons lime juice
- 1 can of Rotel
- corn or flour tortillas and topping

INSTRUCTIONS
1. Cook on LOW for 8 hours with all of the ingredients.
2. NOTES Refrigerate any remaining shredded London broil in a plastic or glass jar. Remember to keep the meat moist by storing it with all of the fluids and sauces.
3. It can be reheat in the microwave or on the stove.
4. You may also freeze leftovers in a freezer-safe container or a plastic bag. Freeze for up to 4 months.

SLOW BEEF SHORT RIBS

PREP TIME:15 MINS.
COOK TIME:8 HOURS
SERVES 8 PEOPLE

- 2 tbsp olive oil
- 1.6kg beef short ribs
- 1 large onion, peeled, sliced
- 3 garlic cloves, peeled, crushed
- 200ml red wine
- 400ml beef stock
- 1 tbsp tomato pureé
- 1 tbsp Worcestershire sauce
- 1 large sprig of thyme
- 2 bay leaves
- Salt and ground black pepper, as desired

METHOD

1. Remove the pot's cover. Set the dial to SEAR/SAUTÉ, the temperature to HI, then hit START/STOP to begin preheating. Allow the device to warm for 5 minutes.
2. Add the oil and short ribs to the pot. Cook, uncovered, for 10 minutes, or until browned on both sides.
3. Add the onions, garlic, red wine, stock, tomato puree, Worcestershire sauce, herbs, salt, and pepper. Stir to mix, then spread sauce over ribs and cover with the lid. To stop cooking, use the START/STOP button.
4. Set the dial to SLOW COOK, the temperature to LO, the timer to 8 hours, and the START/STOP button to begin cooking.

5. When the beef is done, remove the bay leaves and serve it with carrots and creamy mustard mash.

POT ROAST PORK SHOULDER WITH PEPPERS

PREP TIME:15 MINS.
COOK TIME:5H 30 MINS
SERVES 6 PEOPLE

- 2 tbsp olive oil
- 1 x 2kg tied pork shoulder and rolled,
- fat trimmed
- Salt, as desired
- Ground black pepper, as desired
- 2 medium red onions, peeled, finely sliced
- 1 red chili, deseeded and finely chopped
- 4 peppers, mixed colours, deseeded and quartered
- 1 tbsp sweet smoked paprika
- 1 garlic clove, peeled and crushed
- 2 tbsp tomato purée
- 1 x 400g can chopped tomatoes
- 200ml chicken stock
- 2 tbsp fresh sage leaves
- 1 tsp dried fennel seeds

- 1 bay leaf

METHOD
1. Remove the pot's cover. Set the dial to SEAR/SAUTÉ, the temperature to HI, then hit START/STOP to begin preheating. Allow the unit to preheat for 5 minutes.
2. Fill the pot halfway with oil. Season pork and place fat side down. Cook uncovered for 7-10 minutes, then flip the pork over several times to achieve even browning on both sides and cook for another 8-10 minutes. Remove the pork from the the pot and put it aside.
3. Season with onions, chili, peppers, paprika, garlic, tomato purée, diced tomatoes, stock, and herbs to taste. Stir everything together and heat for 5 minutes, or until softened. Return the pork to rest on the veggies. Cover with the lid after spooning the sauce over the pork. To stop cooking, press START/STOP.
4. Set the dial to SLOW COOK, the temperature to HI, the timer to 5 hours, and the START/STOP button to start cooking.
5. Check the pork for doneness after 45 minutes. If not, flip the pork over and continue cooking.
6. When the pork is done, gently remove the cover and let it cool for 5 minutes before slicing and serving.

LAMB WITH PUY LENTILS

PREP TIME:15 MINS.
TOTAL TIME:8H 15 MINS
SERVES 6 PEOPLE

- 1.3kg approx. half leg of lamb
- 2 garlic cloves, peeled, finely sliced
- 2-3 sprigs of rosemary
- To taste salt and ground black pepper
- 4 echalion shallots, peeled, halved
- 190ml red wine
- 300ml lamb or chicken stock
- 1 tbsp sundried tomato purée
- 200g dried puy lentils, rinsed, drained
- 2 bay leaves

METHOD

1. Make small slits all over the lamb and load them with garlic slices and rosemary sprigs. Season lamb to taste.
2. Remove the pot's cover. Add shallots, red wine, stock, tomato purée, lentils, bay leaves, salt, and pepper to taste. Stir to mix, then add lamb to the pot on top of the lentils. Cover with a lid after spooning the liquid over the lamb.
3. Set the dial to SLOW COOK, the temperature to LO, the time to 8 hours, and the START/STOP button to begin cooking.

4. After 4 hours, lift the top and immediately flip the lamb over, scraping any lentils back into liquid.
5. When the lamb is done cooking, slice it and serve it with lentils.

MUSTARD CHICKEN WITH MUSHROOMS AND LEEKS

PREP TIME:10 MINS.
COOK TIME:55 MINS.
SERVES 4 PEOPLE

- 1kg bone in, skin on chicken thighs
- 1 tbsp olive oil
- 2 shallots, peeled, finely sliced
- 2 garlic cloves, peeled and minced
- 400g leeks, cleaned and cut into 5cm slices
- 200g chestnut mushrooms, wiped and sliced
- 200ml white wine
- 1 tbsp Dijon mustard
- 400ml chicken stock
- 150ml low fat crème fraîche
- 2 tbsp fresh tarragon

METHOD

1. Preheat for 2-3 minutes, or until hot. Remove any extra fat from the chicken and season with salt and pepper, and add the oil. Sauté the chicken skin side down for 10 minutes, or until the skin is golden and crisp. It should be cooked for another 5 minutes after flipping the chicken.
2. Remove chicken from pan and set aside. Before adding leeks, mushrooms, and garlic cook for 2 minutes. Then, Cook for 5 minutes. Allow the wine to deglaze the pan's surface and decrease. Stir in the stock, mustard, crème fraiche, and half of the tarragon. Allow to boil for 5 minutes, after then turn off the heat.
3. Return the chicken, skin side up. Cook for 20-25 minutes.
4. Remove the chicken and veggies from the pan and top with the remaining tarragon.Serve with mashed and green veggies.

ONE POT CHICKEN & RED RICE PILAF

PREP TIME:25 MINS.
COOK TIME:1 HOUR.
SERVES 4 PEOPLE

- 2 tbsp olive oil
- 1 bunch of spring onions,
- sliced into 1cm lengths
- 1 red pepper, deseeded, diced into 1cm cubes
- 2 garlic cloves, peeled, crushed
- 1 tsp ground cinnamon
- 1 tsp ground coriander

- 1 tsp ground cumin
- 200g red rice, rinsed, drained
- 500ml chicken stock, warm
- 75g dried apricots, halved
- 25g coriander leaves, chopped (reserve some leaves for garnish)
- 4 x 275g bone in, skin on chicken legs
- Salt, as desired
- Ground black pepper, as desired

METHOD

1. Preheat the oven to 180°C. Allow oil to heat for 2 to 3 minutes.
2. When the pan is heated, add the spring onions and pepper. Sauté for 2 minutes, then add the garlic, ground cinnamon, coriander, and cumin. Cook for 5 minutes, or until the onions and peppers have softened.
3. Stir in the rice, stock, apricots, and coriander leaves. Season the chicken legs skin side up on top of the rice. Cover the pan with a cover.
4. Cook, covered, for 1 hour. After 1 hour, take the cover from the pan and heat the oven to 220°C. Cook for another 25 to 30 minutes, or until the rice is tender and the chicken is golden brown.
5. It should be removed from oven and set aside for 5 minutes to cool. Serve rice with chicken. Garnish with coriander leaves if desired.

SLOW COOKED VEGGIE CHILLI

**PREP TIME:20 MINS.
TOTAL TIME:4 HOURS.
SERVES 4 PEOPLE**

- 2 tablespoons olive oil
- 1 medium onion peeled, finely chopped
- 1 red pepper, deseeded and diced
- 1 green pepper, deseeded and diced
- 2 garlic cloves, peeled, minced
- 1 teaspoon chilli powder
- 1 teaspoon cumin powder
- 1 teaspoon coriander
- 1 teaspoon smoked paprika
- 1 teaspoon oregano
- 500g sweet potato, cut into 2cm chunks
- 1 tablespoon tomato purée
- 1 can (400g) chopped tomatoes
- 1 can (400g) red kidney beans, drained and rinsed
- 1 can (400g) black beans, drained and rinsed
- 450ml vegetable stock
- Salt and freshly ground black pepper as desired

METHOD
1. To start cooking, choose SEAR/SAUTÉ, set to HI-5, then hit START/STOP. Heat for 2 minutes with olive oil.
2. Cook for 10 minutes, or until the onions and peppers are tender. Stir once.
3. Stir in the garlic, spices, sweet potato, tomato purée, chopped tomatoes, beans, stock, and season with salt and pepper to taste. To select cooking, use the START/STOP button.
4. Close the lid, choose SLOW COOK, and set the temperature to HIGH for 3 hours and 30 minutes. To start cooking, press START/STOP.
5. Check after 3 hours to see whether the potato is done; if not, simmer for another 30 minutes.
6. When the chili is done, gently remove it from the pot and serve it hot with guacamole, crusty bread, and coriander leaves.

SLOW COOKED RAGU

PREP TIME:15 MINS.
TOTAL TIME:3H 15 MINS.
SERVES 4 PEOPLE

- Cooked pasta
- 500g ground beef
- 2-3 carrots, chopped
- 2 celery sticks, chopped
- 1 onion, chopped
- 2 x cans chopped tomatoes

- 2 tbsp tomato puree
- 2 garlic cloves
- Fresh rosemary
- 1 x cup water
- 1 tsp red paprika
- 1/3 tsp chilli powder
- Bay leaf
- Salt & pepper
- Oil for frying
- Parmesan and butter for serving
- 50g butter

METHOD
1. In the foodi cooking pot, use the sear setting on medium heat and add 3 tbsp of oil and chopped onion. Fry until softened.
2. Then, Add the meat and cook for 3-4 minutes.
3. Apart from the butter, combine the other ingredients.
4. Close the lid. Set it to slow cooking on low for 3-4 hours.
5. After the slow cooking is finished, add the butter. Mix thoroughly and cook for 10 minutes on the sear program.
6. In the meantime, prepare your favorite pasta.
7. Serve immediately with freshly shaved Parmesan and fresh basil.

DATE TAGINE WITH COUSCOUS AND SLOW COOKED SPICED DUCK AND 'QUACKLING'

PREP TIME:20 MINS.
TOTAL TIME:5H 20 MINS.
SERVES 2 PEOPLE

- 2 Duck legs, skin removed and saved
- 2 tsp vegetable oil
- 1 white onion
- 1 aubergine
- 2 garlic cloves
- 1 small red chilli, deseeded thumb-sized piece ginger
- 1/2 tbsp cumin
- 1/2 tbsp coriander powder
- 1/2 tbsp cinnamon
- ½ tsp ginger powder
- 1 lemon, pulp and pith scooped out and discarded
- 100g de-stoned dates
- 200ml passata
- 100ml water
- 50g blanched almonds, chopped
- ½ tin of chickpeas
- Bulgur wheat to serve
- Dollop natural/Greek style yoghurt to serve
- Fresh mint to serve

METHOD

1. Remove the skin off the duck legs gently. Wrap it in cling film and store it in the fridge for later. This will be used later to produce the crispy 'quackling'.
2. Use the SAUTE/SEAR function (high heat setting) to brown the duck legs for a few minutes.
3. While the duck is frying, blitz the white onion, garlic, chili, ginger, spices, and preserved lemon into a thick paste in a food processor.
4. Set aside the browned duck. Still using the SAUTE/SEAR function (high heat setting), heat the oil and fry the spice paste for 5 minutes, carefully stirring occasionally.
5. While the spice paste is heating, add half the dates in a food processor with 100ml of water until smooth. Cut the remaining dates into bits.
6. When the spice paste has cooked, add the dates (both pureed and pieces), passata, chickpeas, and chopped coriander. Stir in the duck legs. Insert the Digital Cooking Probe into the thickest part of the meat.
7. Close the cover and set the Slow Cooking setting to high for 3 hours or medium for 5 hours, stirring periodically.
8. When the duck has an hour remaining, chop the aubergine into big cubes and add to the multi-cooker, stirring to cover in the sauce and juices.
9. When the duck has 20 minutes remaining, remove the skin from the fridge set it flat, and spread out on some parchment paper. Sprinkle with rock salt and grill over medium heat until the skin is browned and crispy. (Tip: the skin will always get crisper after being removed from the heat and let to cool somewhat).
10. Serve with bulgur wheat and your favorite chopped veggies, spread the 'quackling' over the top,and finish with a dollop of natural yogurt and mint.

PULLED PORK SLOPPY JOES

PREP TIME:10 MINS.
TOTAL TIME:10 HOURS.
SERVES 8 PEOPLE

- 1kg pork lion or pork tenderloin
- 3/4 cup vegetable stock
- 1 cup bbq sauce (homemade or store bought)
- 2 tbsp olive oil
- 2 cloves of garlic
- 1 tbsp honey
- Bay leaf
- Salt and pepper
- 1/2 tsp chilli powder
- Burger buns to serve

METHOD

1. Season the meat with salt and pepper and let it aside for 5 minutes to rest.
2. Arrange the meat in the foodi.
3. Mix together the remaining ingredients.
4. Select the slow cooking method. Set the temperature to medium and the timer to 8-10 hours.
5. When the time is up. Shred the meat using forks.
6. Serve on sandwiches, wraps or even baked potatoes.

SLOW COOKED LAMB WITH LAYERED VEGETABLES

PREP TIME:20 MINS. **COOK TIME3 HOURS**
SERVES 4 PEOPLE

- 600g potatoes, peeled and finely sliced
- 300g sweet potatoes, peeled and finely sliced
- 2 onions, finely sliced
- 3 carrots, sliced
- 2 garlic cloves, crushed
- 2-3 thyme sprigs
  freshly ground black pepper and salt
- 500ml chicken or vegetable stock
- 1.5kg half shoulder of lamb

METHOD
1. Preheat the oven to 160°C.
2. In the Ninja Possible pot, layer the veggies, garlic, thyme, and spices.
3. Pour over chicken or vegetable stock. Place lamb on top. Season to taste. Cover with lid.
4. Put the pot in the preheated oven. After 1½ hours, gently remove the cover from the pot and place it back in the oven. Cook for an additional 1½ hours, or until the lamb is tender.
5. Serve hot with green vegetables.

TOMATO & BASIL LINGUINE

PREP TIME:10 MINS.
TOTAL TIME:23 MINS
SERVES 4 PEOPLE

- 350g linguine
- 350g cherry tomatoes, halved
- 1 medium onion, sliced
- ¼ tsp chilli flakes
- 3 garlic cloves, sliced
- 8 basil leaves, roughly chopped, plus extra to serve
- 2 tsp salt
- 1/2 tsp ground black pepper
- 1.5L cold water
- Parmesan cheese or vegetarian equivalent, grated to serve
- Extra Virgin olive Oil, to serve

METHOD

1. In the Ninja Possible Pot, place linguine, cherry tomatoes, sliced onion, chilli flakes, sliced garlic, basil, salt and pepper, and water. and select BRAISE on HI
2. Bring to a boil (around 5-6 minutes), stirring with tongs. Allow to cook for 10-13 minutes, or until the pasta is al dente with a tiny quantity of liquid left.
3. Serve immediately in bowls topped with a splash of olive oil, basil leaves and Parmesan cheese.

DESSERT, SNACKS & APPETIZERS

CHOCOLATE SPONGE PUDDING

PREP TIME: 15 MINS.
COOK TIME: 20 MINS.
SERVES 4 PEOPLE

- 225g butter, softened, plus extra for greasing
- 300g soft light brown sugar, divided
- 4 large eggs
- 1 tsp vanilla extract
- 75ml milk
- 175g self-rising flour
- 75g cocoa powder, divided, plus extra for dusting
- 2 tsp baking powder
- 250ml boiling water
- Whipped cream or ice cream, to serve

METHOD
1. The inside of the pot should be grease with butter.
2. In a large mixing bowl, combine the butter, 225g brown sugar, eggs, vanilla extract, and milk. Sift together the flour, 40g cocoa, and baking powder.
3. Mix all ingredients by hand for 2 to 3 minutes, or 1 to 2 minutes if using a hand mixer on medium speed.

4. Spoon the mixture into the pot and smooth it up with a spatula.
5. In a small dish, combine 35g cocoa powder, 75g sugar, and 250ml boiling water. Mix well. Pour the chocolate mixture over the pudding mixture.
6. To begin cooking, set the dial to BAKE, the temperature to 180°C, the timer to 20 minutes, and the START/STOP button.
7. When a cocktail stick placed into the center comes out clean, the cooking is done. it should be served hot with whipped cream or ice cream.

CHEESE & CHIVE SCONES

PREP TIME:5 MINS.
TOTAL TIME:35 MINS.
SERVES 4 PEOPLE

- 270g plain flour
- 6g baking powder
- ½ tsp salt
- 1 tbsp chives, finely chopped
- 40g mature cheddar, grated
- 1 egg
- 100g butter, softened
- 60g crème fraiche
- 1 egg & 1 tbsp milk for brushing

METHOD

1. In a large mixing bowl, combine the flour, baking powder, salt, chives, and cheddar. Mix thoroughly, then add the egg, softened butter, and crème fraiche. Combine as well as possible, then put

on a clean surface and knead just until all loose flour has been incorporated into the dough. You don't want to overwork the dough since scones should be flaky and buttery.
2. Select BAKE, 170°C, and 17 minutes. To begin preheating, press the START/STOP button.
3. Roll out the dough to about 3cm thickness while the unit is preheating. Cut out scones using a biscuit cutter, then rework leftover dough and cut again.
4. Combine the egg and milk in a small bowl. The scones should be brushed with the egg mixture.
5. When the machine beeps to indicate that it has warmed, gently spray the pot with cooking spray and add the scones. To start cooking, close the hood.
6. When the scones are done, take them from the oven and set them aside to cool. Serve with butter, chutney, or as a side dish to soups and stews.

CHOCOLATE ORANGE BROWNIE PIE

PREP TIME:PT0H1H.
TOTAL TIME:1H 32 MINS.
SERVES16 PEOPLE

For the pie crust
- 225g ground almonds
- 200g arrowroot flour
- 175g salted grass-fed organic butter, cubed
- 2 tbsp raw cane sugar
- 1 large Juice and zest of orange

For the brownie batter
- 175g unsalted grass-fed organic butter, cubed
- 140g 90% dark chocolate, roughly chopped
- 140g ground almonds
- 35g cacao powder
- 1/2 tsp sea salt
- 4 large eggs
- 100g raw cane sugar
- 100g coconut sugar
- 1 tbsp orange extract
- 1/2 tsp vanilla extract

METHOD
1. Except for the orange juice, combine all of the pie crust ingredients in a food processor and pulse until the mixture resembles breadcrumbs. Add a spoonful of orange juice at a time until the dough barely comes together into a ball. Wrap the dough in clingfilm and place it in the freezer for 30 minutes, or until firm.
2. Preheat the oven to 180°C.
3. Knuckle pie crust dough into the Impossible Pan, working it up to just below the rivets. Make sure the sides are somewhat thicker than the base. Prick the base with a fork. Chill the dough in the pan in the freezer for 10 minutes, or in the refrigerator for 30 minutes.
4. Line the pan with paper, allowing it to extend over the edges, and then fill with baked beans. Blind bake for 10-15 minutes, then remove the beans and bake for another 10 minutes.
5. Melt the butter and chocolate in a double boiler and set aside to cool slightly.
6. In a medium mixing dish, add ground almonds, cacao powder, and sea salt.

7. In a large mixing bowl, whisk together the eggs, sugars, orange essence, and vanilla extract until thick. When the mixture falls off the whisk, it should create ribbons.
8. Stir in the melted chocolate mixture until combined, then fold in the dry ingredients until just combined.
9. Bake for 12 minutes after pouring the brownie ingredients into the pie shell. Cooking is finished when the outside 2" of batter comes out with a few crumbs on a toothpick.
10. Remove from the oven and set aside to cool fully before cutting into wedges. With vanilla ice cream, coconut yogurt, or whipped coconut cream, serve hot or cold.

Notes

Pie may be kept in an airtight container in the refrigerator for up to 1 week or in the freezer for up to 6 weeks. If frozen, Thaw in the refrigerator overnight.

Raw cane sugar can be substituted in equal parts with an erythritol and stevia sugar substitute or more coconut sugar.

GREEN TOMATOES CHUTNEY

PREP TIME:15 MINS.
TOTAL TIME:4H 15 MINS.
SERVES 12 PEOPLE

- 1 cup apple cider vinegar
- 1 cup light brown sugar
- 1.5 kg green tomatoes, finely sliced
- 60 g prunes, chopped
- 1.2 kg red onions, finely sliced
- 5 cloves garlic, minced

- 2 apples, finely sliced
- 1 red chili, seeded and finely chopped
- 2 tsp coriander seeds
- Salt and black pepper
- Optional star arise and cumin seeds if you like the flavour

METHOD
1. Set the Ninja cooker to slow cooking mode on high.
2. The cider vinegar should be poured into the slow cooker pot and add the sugar. Stir well until the sugar melts.
3. Mix together the remaining ingredients. Cook for 3-4 hours with the lid on.
4. Check on the chutney every few hours and give it a good stir to ensure it cooks evenly. If there is still too much liquid in the cooker after 3 hours, remove the cover and cook for another 30 minutes without the lid on so the liquid may evaporate.
5. Transfer the chutney to prepared jars.
6. Keep in the fridge for up to a month.

GLUTEN-FREE PAN PIZZA

PREP TIME:1H 45 MINS.
TOTAL TIME:1H 57 MINS
SERVES 8 PEOPLE

For the dough
- 355g gluten-free self-raising flour
- 1 tsp active dried yeast
- 1 tsp sea salt
- 1/2 tsp dried oregano

- 1/2 tsp garlic powder
- 50g natural yoghurt or coconut yoghurt
- 2 tbsp olive oil
  (plus extra for proofing/cooking)
- 150ml tepid milk or water

For the topping
- 150-175ml pizza sauce
- 175g grated cheddar and mozzarella, divided
- 45g grated parmesan or pecorino
- 1/3 green pepper, sliced
- 1/3 red pepper, sliced
- 1/3 large red onion, finely sliced
- 1 tbsp sliced black olives
- 1 tbsp tinned sweetcorn kernels
- 1 tsp fresh basil, finely chopped
- 1 tsp fresh oregano, finely chopped
- Small handful torn fresh basil leaves

METHOD
1. Stir together all of the dry pizza dough ingredients until well combined. Mix in the yogurt, olive oil, and dry ingredients. Stir in the milk gradually until you have a smooth, lump-free dough. Form the dough into a ball and set it in the pan, sprinkle with olive oil, and cover with a moist tea towel or cling film. Allow to proof until doubled in size, up to 1 hour.
2. Uncover the dough and sprinkle with a little extra olive oil. Using your fingers, flatten the dough into a uniform layer in the pan. Then, Cover and allow to proof for another 30 minutes.
3. Preheat the oven to 245°C.
4. Spread the pizza sauce over the pizza with the back of a spoon, leaving 1 cm around the edges. Sprinkle with the cheeses,

reserving 45g of the shredded cheddar and mozzarella. Top with the sliced veggies, black olives, and sweetcorn kernels. Then, Sprinkle with the remaining herbs and cheese.

5. Cook for 2 minutes on high before transferring to the oven and baking for 12 to 18 minutes. Remove from the oven and slide a butter knife or silicone spatula over the sides of the pan to loosen any stuck cheese.
6. Allow to cool for 5 minutes before sprinkling with torn fresh basil leaves gently transferring to a chopping board and slicing into 8 wedges.

Notes:
The chopped fresh herbs may be substituted with 1/4 tsp dry herbs.

SLOW COOKED MULLED WINE

PREP TIME:5 MINS.
TOTAL TIME:1H 5 MINS.
SERVES 2 PEOPLE

- 1 litter of red wine, such as Cabernet Sauvignon or Merlot
- 1/2 cup of spiced rum
- 5 tbsp honey or maple shroud
- 5-6 whole cloves
- 5 cardamom seeds
- 4 whole star anise pods
- 2 cinnamon sticks
- 1/2 cup of orange juice

- 1 orange cut in slices
- 1 vanilla stick

METHOD
1. In a slow cooker, combine all ingredients.
2. Set foodi to low. Cook for about 1 hour on low heat.
3. When the timer goes off, fill each mug up with hot wine.
4. Garnish with fresh cranberries, orange slices, and so forth.
5. Make it vegan by switching maple syrup for honey. You may even add additional sweetness if desired. If you don't like rum, try some brandy instead. You may also prepare this ahead of time and reheat it later.

PORTUGUESE PROTEIN RICE PUDDING

PREP TIME:15 MINS.
TOTAL TIME:4H 15 MINS.
SERVES 2 PEOPLE

Part 1
- 100ml coconut milk
- 1 tbsp butter
- 75g vanilla whey protein

Part 2
- Skin from 1/2 lemon
- 1 cinnamon stick
- 5 tbsp Stevia
- 600ml coconut milk

- 100g rice pudding rice
- Pinch of pink Himalayan salt
- 3 egg yolks
- ground cinnamon

METHOD
1. Part one: Place the milk, butter, and whey protein in the tiny cup of your NINJA KITCHEN SYSTEM and pulse to blend.
2. Stir together the whey mixture, lemon skin, cinnamon stick, stevia, coconut milk, rice, and salt in the pot of your NINJA FOODI.
3. Place the cover on the NINJA FOODI, choose SLOW cook on LOW, and cook for 4 hours, stirring periodically.
4. When the rice pudding is done, add the egg yolks and stir to combine.
5. Remove the cinnamon stick and lemon skin and serve with ground cinnamon.

SPICY CARROT CHUTNEY

PREP TIME:30 MINS.
TOTAL TIME:1H 45 MINS
SERVES 3 PEOPLE

- 3 garlic cloves, peeled and minced
- 2 chillies, deseeded and finely chopped
- 50g fresh root ginger, peeled and grated

- 500g carrots, peeled and grated
- 2 apples, peeled, cored and chopped
- 1 onion, peeled and diced
- 300ml white wine vinegar
- 1 tsp dried cumin seeds
- 1 tsp mustard seeds
- 1 tsp salt
- 300g granulated sugar
- 1 tsp dried cumin seeds
- 1 tsp mustard seeds
- 1 tsp salt

METHOD
1. Add garlic, chili, ginger, carrots, apples, onions, vinegar, spices, and salt to the possible pot.
2. Select BRAISE on HI stir in sugar until dissolved, then cover the pot with a lid and bring chutney to a boil before simmering on a LO for approximately an hour until the mixture is thick and carrots are tender. Then steam escapes through vent holes in the lid.
3. Pot into sterilized jam jars. Top with waxed discs and lids.
4. Leave for 2 weeks to mature. Delicious served with cheese

CHEESECAKE

PREP TIME:25 MINS.
CHILLING TIME6 HOURS
TOTAL TIME:1H 55 MINS.
SERVES 8 PEOPLE

For the base
- 80g butter, melted, plus extra for greasing
- 125g digestive biscuits, crushed

For the filling
- 600g full fat cream cheese, room temperature
- 160g caster sugar, divided
- 2 tbsp plain flour
- 1 tsp vanilla bean extract
- 2 large eggs
- 1 lemon, zest and juice, divided
- 300ml sour cream, divided
- 1l water
- To serve fresh berries

METHOD

1. Butter a 20cm springform cake tin. Line the bottom with a large of foil, then clip together so the foil is enclosed and the excess sticks out, then push up the sides.
2. In a medium mixing bowl, combine melted butter and crumbled biscuits. Mix until all of the biscuits are coated. Then spoon and press the biscuits into the prepared tin.

3. In a large mixing bowl, using a hand mixer on low to medium speed, beat the cream cheese with all but 1 tablespoon of sugar and all of the flour for 1 minute.
4. Whisk together the vanilla, eggs, lemon zest, and 1 teaspoon lemon juice in a mixing bowl until smooth. When the mixture is smooth, gently whisk in 140ml sour cream. The top of the cheesecake should be cover with foil.
5. Pour rack and water into the pot. Place the cheesecake on a rack. Cover with a lid. Set the dial to BAKE, the temperature to 120°C, the timer to 90 minutes, and the START/STOP button to begin cooking.
6. When the cheesecake still has a tiny wobble, the cooking is finished. Allow to cool after removing from the pot.
7. In a medium mixing bowl, combine the remaining sour cream, 1 tablespoon caster sugar, and 2 tablespoons lemon juice. Spread over the top of the chilled cheesecake before chilling in the refrigerator for 4 to 6 hours. Please be aware that the cheesecake may crack somewhat; this is usual.
8. Serve in slices with fresh berries.

MEASUREMENT CONVERSION

• Temperature Conversion Chart

Fahrenheit (°F)	Celsius (°C)
200	93
250	121
300	149
350	177
400	204

6. Volume Conversion Chart

Cups	Milliliters (ml)	Liters (L)
1/4	60	0.06
1/3	80	0.08
1/2	120	0.12

2/3	160	0.16
3/4	180	0.18
1	240	0.24
2	480	0.48
3	720	0.72
4	960	0.96
5	1,200	1.20

7. Weight Conversion Chart

Ounces (oz)	Grams (g)	Kilograms (kg)
1	28.35	0.028
2	56.70	0.057
3	85.05	0.085
4	113.40	0.113

5	141.75	0.142
6	170.10	0.170
7	198.45	0.198
8	226.80	0.227
9	255.15	0.255
10	283.50	0.284

Additional Tips:

- However, Use the included measuring cup and spoon for accurate measurements.
- When using liquid ingredients, always measure at eye level to avoid overfilling.
- For dry ingredients, fluff up the ingredient before measuring to ensure an accurate measurement.
- When converting between Fahrenheit and Celsius, remember that there are approximately 5/9 degrees Celsius for every 1 degree Fahrenheit.

Cookbook by Nancy C. Bergstrom

Happy Cooking

BONUS
MEAL PLANNER

Cookbook by Nancy C. Bergstrom

DAILY PLANNER

Date: _____ Month: _____

| Monday | Tuesday | Wednesday |

| Thursday | Friday | Saturday |

| Sunday | Note |

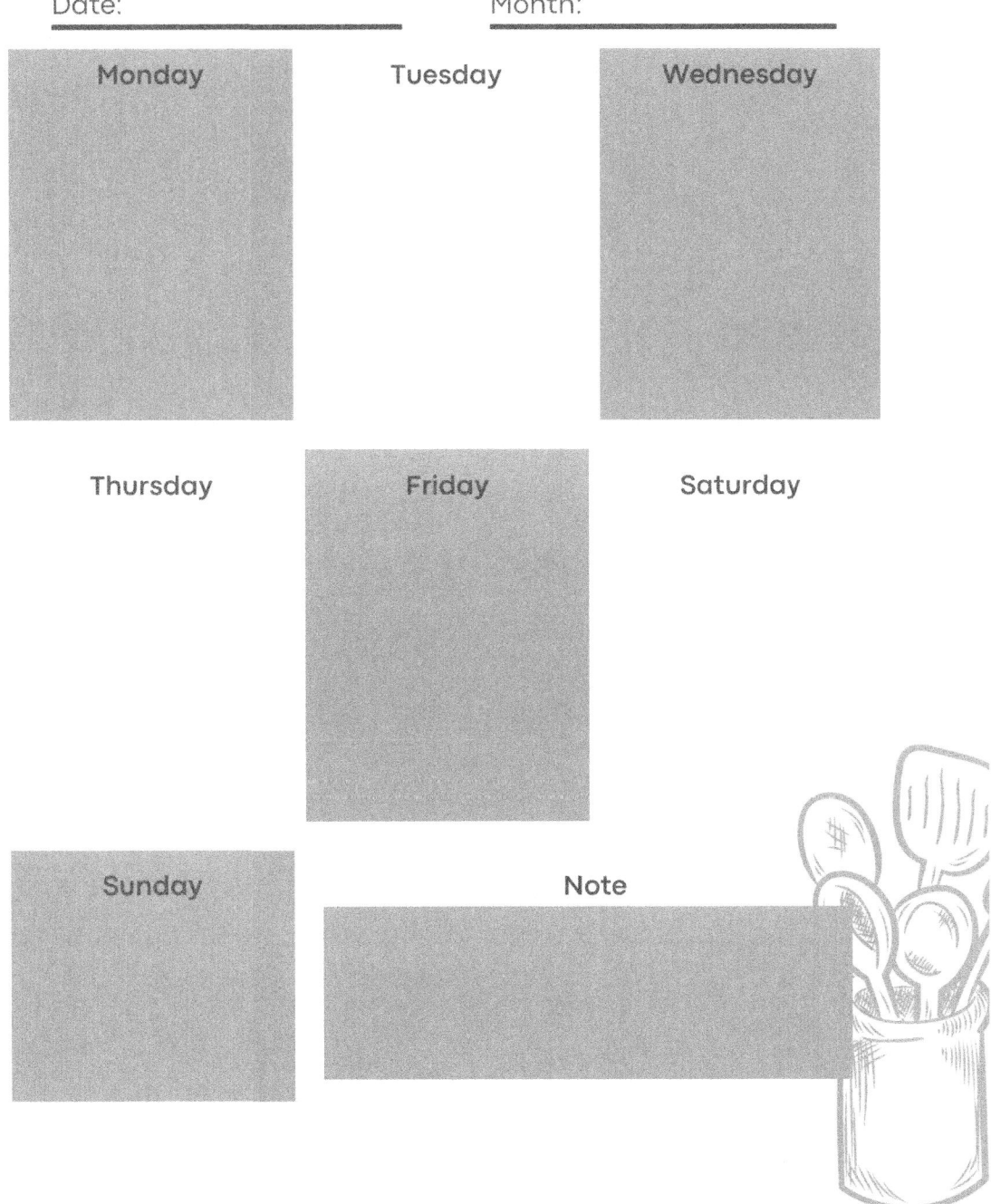

DAILY PLANNER

Date: _____ Month: _____

Monday

Tuesday

Wednesday

Thursday

Friday

Saturday

Sunday

Note

Cookbook by Nancy C. Bergstrom

DAILY PLANNER

Date: _____ Month: _____

| Monday | Tuesday | Wednesday |

| Thursday | Friday | Saturday |

| Sunday | Note |

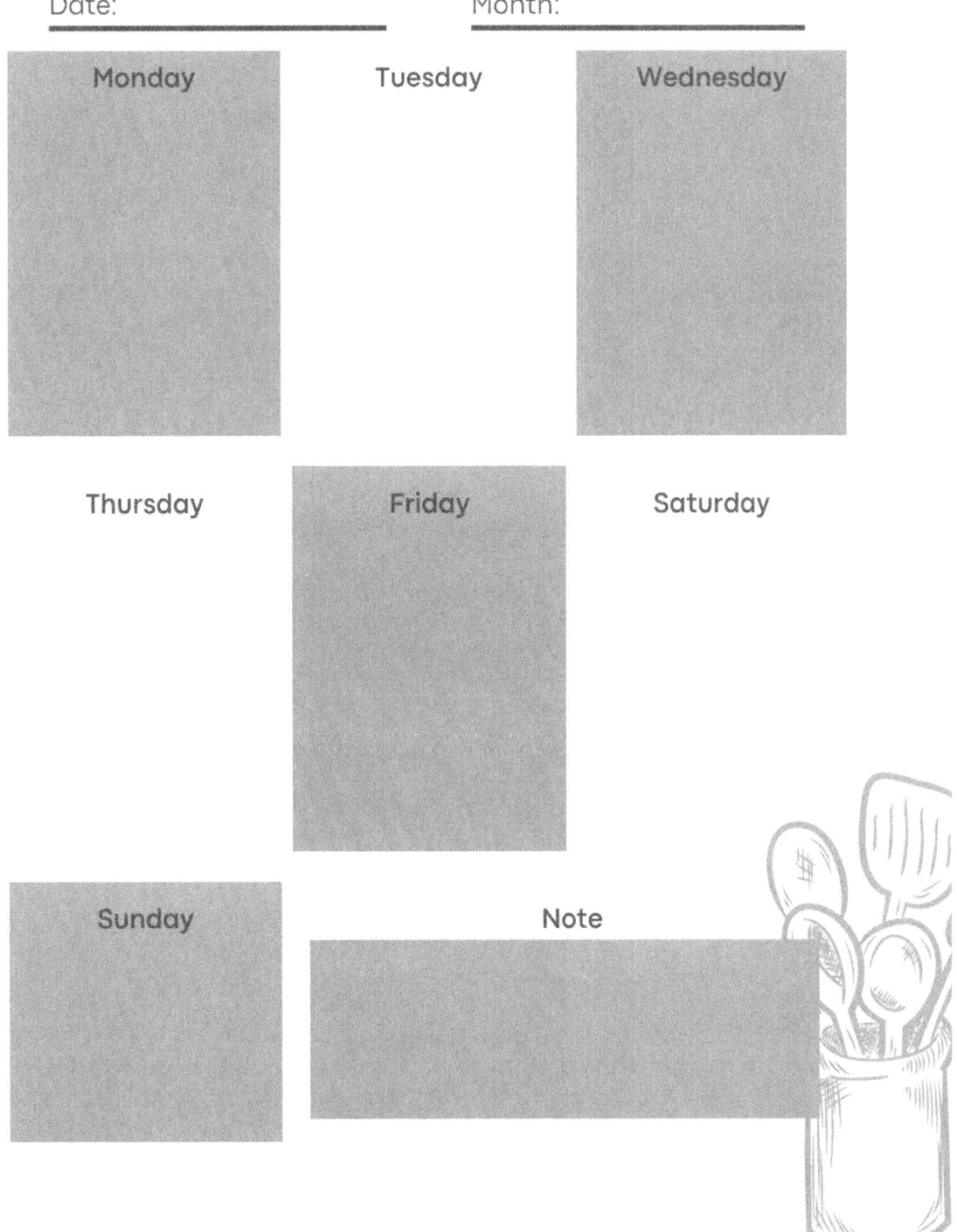

Cookbook by Nancy C. Bergstrom

DAILY PLANNER

Date: _____ Month: _____

Monday

Tuesday

Wednesday

Thursday

Friday

Saturday

Sunday

Note

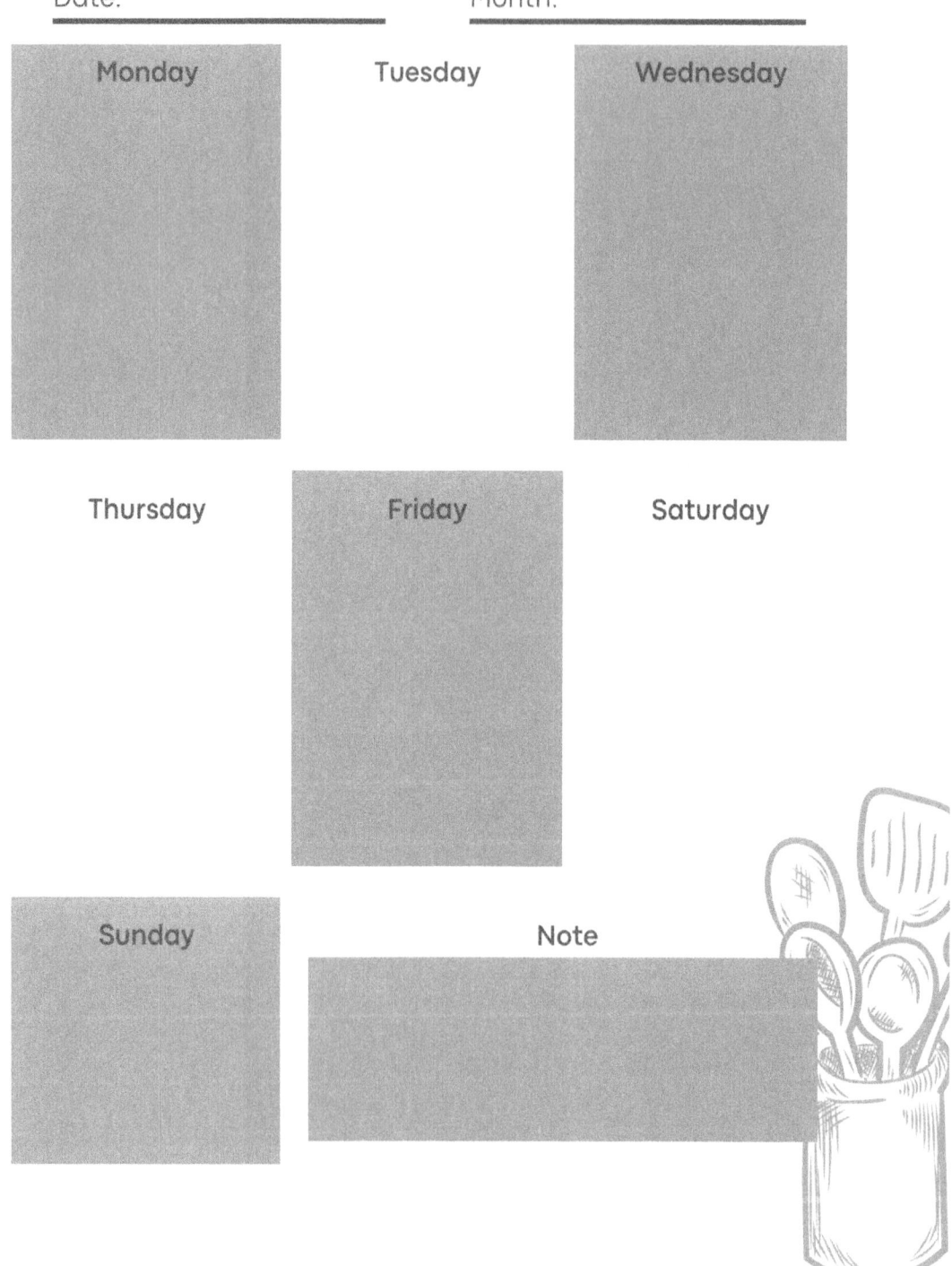

Cookbook by Nancy C. Bergstrom

DAILY PLANNER

Date: _____   Month: _____

| Monday | Tuesday | Wednesday |

| Thursday | Friday | Saturday |

| Sunday | Note |

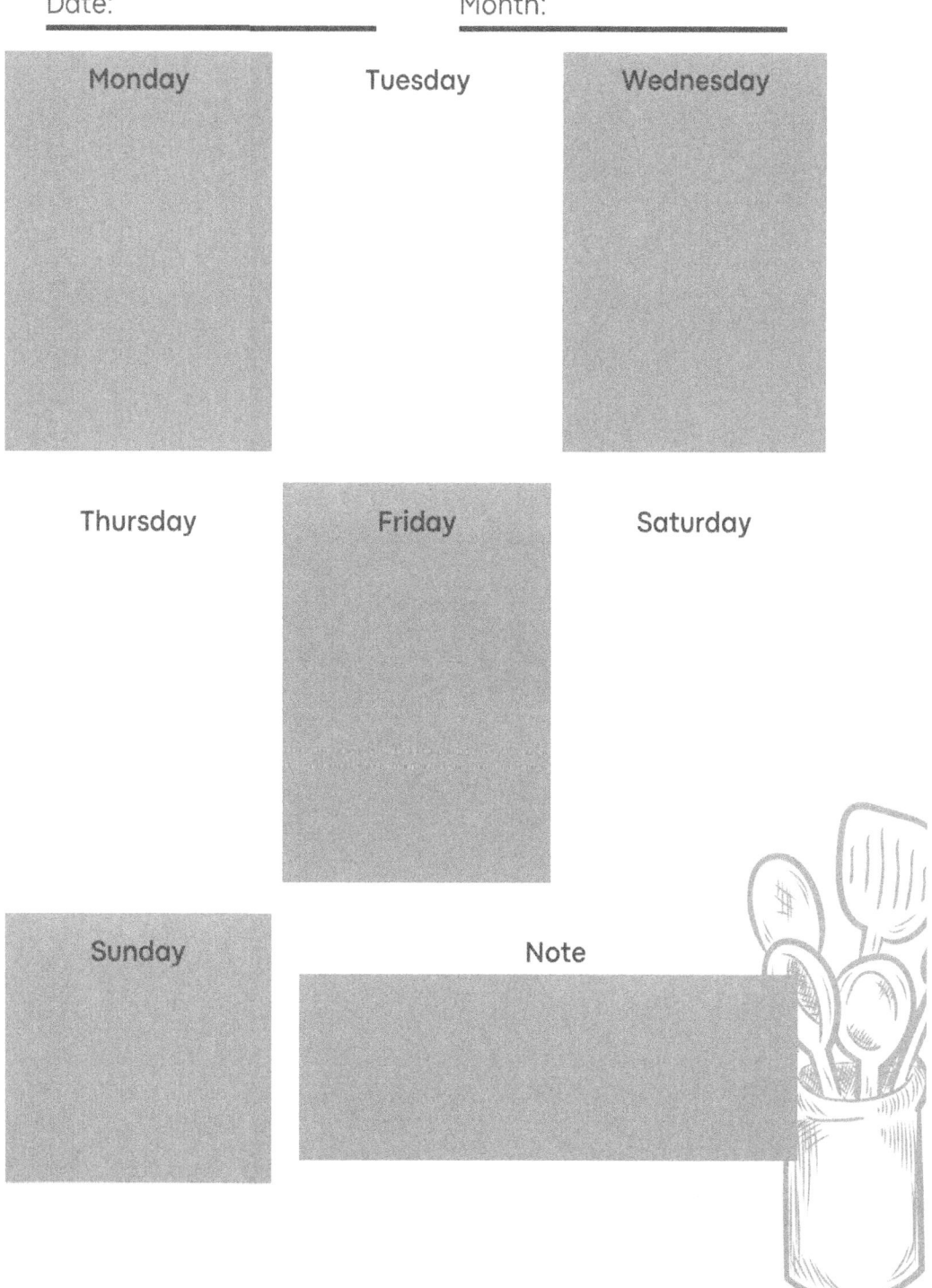

Cookbook by Nancy C. Bergstrom

Printed in Great Britain
by Amazon